Cat Confidence

feline strategies for enjoying life

Library of Congress Control Number: 2010911574
ISBN: Hardcover   978-1-4500-6486-6
       Softcover   978-1-4500-6485-9
       Ebook   978-1-4500-6487-3

CONTENTS

Acknowledgements

I wonder if any book is ever written just by the author. I reckon not. It takes many minds to discuss, suggest, criticise (constructively, of course) and improve the original idea. I am blessed with an amazing family and wonderful friends, so here is a small word of acknowledgement for all their contribution to Thomas's book. I had to do the negotiating on his behalf because he was, generally, otherwise employed, but then that's a cat for you: good even at delegating.

My elder sister, Janet Stonier, edited the manuscript for me. I lost that copy, but managed to retrieve most of her very helpful (and literate) suggestions. My younger sister, Erica Bethke, is also an editor of note, and I thank her for her careful reading.

My grandchildren, Alexandra and James Murphy, read the manuscript quitE early on and Alex made suggestions on where inconsistencies had crept in and where clarity had been lost.

Liz Murphy and Cathy Cowin, my two wonderful daughters were most encouraging and kept me at it when I lost impetus. I owe them a huge debt of gratitude. I also thank my housemate, Lynn Wostenholm for her constant encouragement, patience and understanding, as well as for reading it and hearing about it until she must have been heartily sick of it. Her faith in me really keeps me going.

My friends Diane Holmes, Carol Nieth and John Tidy from our tiny mountain village of Hogsback, helped me with illustrations, providing drawings of cats, especially of Tommy. I hope they will enjoy seeing their beautiful artwork in print as much as I have enjoyed using them.

Various other friends both here in South Africa and overseas, have read the manuscript and encouraged me to go on, promising to buy a copy when it is published. I hold them to that and look forward to signing many, many copies!

Hogsback, July 2010

INTRODUCTION

Thomas lies on his side in feline repose. His head is supported on my yesterday's sweater and he gives the slightest suggestion of a snore. His magnificent black coat has its winter thickness and his white socks and jabot form the outposts of his deeply fluffy white tummy, bulging slightly between his neat paws.

Thomas is not a thin cat.

Thomas is also not a shy cat.

In fact, Thomas has got the world (well HIS world) by the throat and is able to while away the obliging hours in easy relaxation. He has, as far as I can tell, not a care in the world.

When I reach out to stroke him lightly, without opening his eyes, he stretches back and paws and then forms into a slightly rounder shape to continue his nap. The only acknowledgement of my humble service is a little purr.

This book is his. I suspect him to be truly wise, and from time to time discover his huge amber eyes gazing consideringly at me, every line of his furry self expressing his surprise at the incomparable stupidity of the human race.

I'll let him tell it.

CHAPTER 1

Cats choose the up side

My name is Thomas. Tommy. Tom, because that
what I was originally - a tom-cat. Of course, I am not
any more. I suppose you could call me ET – Ex-Tom –
if you wanted to, but I think that would be a kind of
insult. I don't think of myself as an ex-anything. I am
pretty well perfect as I am.

I am beautiful.

I know this because people are forever telling me
so. I have seen myself in the mirror too, and must
confess that my particular pattern of mainly black with

almost-symmetrical white patches is extremely pleasing. My fur is thick and generous and my whiskers long.

I have a nick out of my right ear, not from fighting but by courtesy of the vet who neutered me. You see, I started life as a feral cat, living on the streets, collecting leftovers from the restaurants along the sea front.

I belong to a family of black cats living behind the Dutch Reformed Church in Camps Bay. We were quite a large family, and our numbers grew every year until we were caught and taken to the vet to be 'done'.

These things happen. Life is not something you can totally script yourself. You need to understand that you are dealt a particular hand and what you do with it is up to you. I am not sure that *people* really understand this at all. I hear them all the time, complaining about their lives when they could easily change many aspects of what they have been dealt, if they really wished to. But they don't. Sometimes I suspect that they actually prefer to have problems to compare.

I wonder sometimes if they collect complaints so that they can roll them out and compete with others – "I have a harder time than you!". What a strange notion! And they think they are the peak of creation?

Myself, I have chosen to enjoy life and make the best of every moment. Every cat has a variety of lifestyle choices and I reckon I have made some good ones. I will tell you more about them as we go along.

For a start, once I was no longer going romancing at night, I made the decision to attach myself to permanent feeding. I chose the house next door to the Anglican Church, not far from my birthplace. I had noticed that an elderly cat, Amy, lived there, and she seemed to be quite spoilt.

So I took up residence in the shelter of some thick bushes at the side of the house, and came out from time to time to dash in through the window and munch some of her pellets. They were, without doubt, quite the best I have ever tasted. Expensive, too, I believe. Suits me. I must say, these have made me feel better than ever before.

SHE, who I later discovered was called Margaret, invited me to move in properly, though I was very uncertain about that. I didn't trust her at all. I'd had some pretty poor experiences of people in the past, and I wasn't deliberately going to lay myself open to abuse.

But I could quite clearly see the advantages of being an inside cat, especially in the Cape winter when it rains so much. Summer too, come to think of it, with that insane wind all the time. I get sick and tired of the taste of Table Mountain dust when I bath.

So I allowed myself to be coaxed inside, bit by delicious bit. Mind you, I didn't let her touch me for quite a while, and it was fully two months before I actually purred.

After that I took up residence on her chest where it was good and soft – right under her chin at night - and so I made sure she couldn't move unless I allowed her to. To get back to people. I spend a lot of time watching them and listening to them. Sometimes I sit on one or another's lap so that I can stay right up with the conversation and try to understand better. But as I have just said, they seem to waste so much energy looking for things to be unhappy about.

MF

I know this for a fact because Margaret is a priest – that's why we live next door to the church – and she spends a lot of her time sitting in the lounge listening to people being unhappy. She is much more patient than I think she should be. I think she should tell them straight out that they are wasting their lives; but then she is not a cat, so maybe she doesn't realise that it is mostly their own choice to feel so miserable.

That's where we cats are so good. We know what's going on, and I don't think any of us would purposely choose to find a down side to anything. We put all our effort into finding the up side and then concentrating on that to the exclusion of all else.

Please understand that this is not a matter of the insane positive thinking that some people advocate. We don't pretend that what is nasty is actually the best think ever to happen to us. Not at all. When something is bad, we walk away from it. But what we do try to do is focus on happiness where we can find it. That way we spend our lives enjoying ourselves.

They could learn from us.

CHAPTER 2

Cats rule

Mind you, there are exceptions to everything, I suppose.

Take this nut case from next door for example. She is a remarkably beautiful cat – soft silvery greys in pale stripes, like the sun shining through morning mist, and eyes as blue as the sky over the sea. But mad.

Margaret says she is a bulimic bimbo. I think she's right. She is terrorised by a nasty tom living in the same house, name of Pepe. We call him Peepee because that's what he does. Inside, on the furniture.

Because of him, Isabelle spends much of her day here. I suppose she feels safer here. But she is so tense that she eats our food and then vomits it all up again on various carpets or the wooden floor. Nasty mess. She keeps doing the same things over and over again, even when it makes Margaret cross and she gets chased out.

She is slow to learn, you see, and not quick to work out what's best. For instance, it didn't take me long to discover that "Get down!" in a loud voice meant I had to jump off the table pretty promptly, so I was able to shortcut undignified departures. Isabelle, however, never worked that one out. Her departures are pretty well always undignified. I don't think she is a happy cat.

.

She is an exception to the rule of Cats Are Tops. Generally speaking, we are an optimistic bunch.

Not so most people. Another thing I have noticed is that they spend a lot of energy worrying about what MIGHT happen, instead of getting to grips with what is.

I mean, imagine lying awake at night when you could be sleeping, all because you want to imagine what would happen if the wheels fell off your life. I can't even

contemplate wasting good sleeping time doing that!
What do they think they will gain by this?

When they come to consult Margaret, they are all irritable and short-tempered. I try to comfort them and calm them down, but they push me away, get up, and walk up and down saying the same kind of things over and over. Like, "What if I lose my job?"; "What if they retrench me after all?"; "I would lose my car and then how would I be able to get any work, or do anything?" Silly, really. It hasn't happened so there is nothing they can do about it yet. If the wheels do fall off, they can make a plan to sort something out.

Now cats are confident about the future, because we know that, whatever happens, we will make a plan one way or another.

And we are quite creative when it comes to plans. We're always ready to change the plan at a moment's notice if we can see that things would be more advantageous another way. We don't get so stuck on one way of doing, one way of looking at things.

If I find that attention to my comfort has diminished in this house, I simply move on till I find someone who will look after my needs better. Nothing personal – just common sense.

If I am up on the roof and want to come down, I look at the way I came up and if I find that is not a good way to go down again, then I wander all over looking for a better, safer way. If all else fails, I am not too proud to meow and screech until I get help.

And I always do.

CHAPTER 3

Cats adapt

This makes me think of that other crazy thing that people say that wastes their time and energy: "If only ..."

I don't understand this at all. They do something and it goes wrong. Then, instead of trying something else, they sit there and say, "If only I had done this..." or, "If only that had happened." They often get together and have a competition to see who can think of the most if-only's and that makes them more and more upset. This can go on for hours.

When something really sad happens, like someone dying, they often use this to comfort themselves as well, but of course it doesn't work at all. It's certainly not going to change anything. One will say, "If only I had visited him..." or, "If only we hadn't had that fight..." Then the other person will say, "Don't say that! You can't undo what happened!" which sounds like good sense to me, but the first one just starts crying again.

We cats don't think like that at all. We allow ourselves to be surprised by life. We have the kind of attitude which says, "Oh! Is that what has happened? Well, now let me think of how I can turn this to my advantage. Perhaps I can make a plan to use the experience to learn a new skill, or avoid a similar thing next time. Perhaps I can use this as a trigger to bring about a big change in my life. That would also be positive. Perhaps I can just enjoy this!"

We are clever, you see.

I mean, why waste all the disappointment or pain of this experience by not allowing anything worthwhile to come of it? After all, life is about learning and growing and getting better at being, isn't it?

19

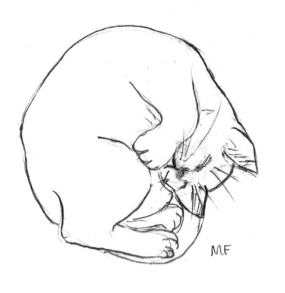

There are some people who understand this. One man, a professor of something, was talking about intelligence to a meeting of the

University of the Third Age at our church (I like to attend these very interesting meetings). He said that one of the prime measures of intelligence is the ability to see patterns in things and learn from events – to adjust one's behaviour in terms of the patterns of life that you have discerned.

That's why I say cats are intelligent (with the odd exception - like Isabelle) unlike many people. Some of them **are** intelligent, I know, and they do learn from their mistakes, but an awful lot of them just go right on, making the same mistakes over and over, and then getting upset and angry about the outcome. You'd think they would recognise the pattern of what they are doing and understand that the same action usually brings about the same result.

They seem to need to find someone or something to blame for what goes wrong and appear to have no sense of random events in life. I wonder what difference it would make if they did find someone to blame for their bad luck? Would it make it less painful? Easier to bear? Would it put it right in some magic way? I think it just gives them a focus for their helpless rage – and can destroy some happy relationships, too.

Apportioning blame is hardly a positive thing to do, and in my view at least, entirely unhelpful. Rather get on with finding a good way forward, searching for a possible happy outcome.

That's what a cat would do.

CHAPTER 4

Cats know what they want

Now here's another thing. Cats go for what they want.

We have two ways of doing this. Either we let people know what we want so that they can get it for us, or we just get it ourselves, whether anyone thinks it a good idea or not.

There is no confusion for people when a cat wants something. We set up a meowing that doesn't stop till we succeed in our quest. If that fails, we have been known to use claws in attack mode to make sure the person concerned is paying attention. But we don't like to do that much – it is a poor investment in the future. Generally we ask, then if that doesn't work, we pile on the behaviour clues and even use manipulation, at which we are absolute geniuses.

Let me illustrate this.

There is a particular brand of very expensive catfood only available at vets. I like it, and I wish to eat it, every day, without exception - several times a day, in fact. Every now and then Margaret gets the idea into her head that there may be something else less expensive and just as nice for me to eat. She tries it out, putting it in my bowl and telling me she has a special treat for me. I'm not stupid. I know that tone of voice.

It is thick with guilt and wheedling, and I am immediately alerted to a possible scam.

I ignore the food. I sit with my back to her and gaze at it, without moving. I look hungry and sad. I gaze some more. As soon as I hear her footsteps, I take up my position in front of the bowl with a rigid back and sad shoulders, and gaze and gaze. I don't eat.

I can go on for days like this if necessary, because I know that she will give in. She will worry about my survival, and eventually weaken and put down the right stuff. Then I eat enough for ten cats. She knows now not even to try anything new.

We cats know how to get what we want. It's just a question of a temporary sacrifice and being prepared to wait it out. The one who can wait longest always wins. And if you can put in a good tragic performance at the same time, you are definitely a winner.

People give up too soon (then blame the other person). A little sacrifice, a little waiting and delayed gratification can win you your heart's desire.

Of course there are sometimes things that you want that are not offered to you. That's when you have to use some initiative.

I've got this pretty well aced as well. I have discovered how to open cupboard doors by hooking my claws into the crack and tugging until the door moves a little, then hooking the whole paw in and pulling. That way you can get at cool secret sleeping places as well as possible sources of delight..

If there is a cloth over something delectable (did she really think we couldn't smell it through the cloth?), then it's an easy matter to lift the edge with a claw and get the nose in. Once the nose has found a way under the covering, the whole head can follow and we've got it!

When someone is eating something delicious, we cats sit up close and purr suggestively. Sometimes we lift our noses, sniff the air delicately in an appreciative way and fix our eyes on the food. Hint, hint! It doesn't always work, but it can score you nice little morsels sometimes, and almost always the left-overs in your bowl. Charm is a great tool and we are past masters.

Another of my tools is a particularly heart-wrenching meow that I have perfected. It always get an instant response, and I keep it for special occasions when nothing else works, or when I can't find her. It can melt the hardest heart.

Now when *people* want something, they don't seem to know how to ask for it. Instead of asking straight out, they seem to spend much of their time hoping someone will notice them and think of offering them what they want. I think they expect others to read their minds. It's so much easier for everyone concerned if you just ask. Of course, the others are always free to say no, but you are just as free to go on asking till you have worn them down.

I've seen Margaret carrying loads of hymn books or putting out chairs and getting really angry because no one helped her. But she didn't ask for help! Why?

The big truth is that people are not good at reading others' minds. They play this little game of "Guess what it is that I really want. I won't give you any clues, and I won't answer your questions truthfully, but I will punish you if you get it wrong."

I have heard them at it.

"Let me help you with that."

"No, no, I can manage fine!"

Then a big sulk because they other person didn't "lift a finger to help when they KNEW I was battling!"

Funny people! It would be a much easier world if they were all cats, or told the truth about their needs and wants.

After all, it doesn't hurt to ask, does it?

CHAPTER 5

Cat baths

I have heard it said that cats have no social graces (this is manifestly untrue – even if we do like to put our bottoms in people's faces). It may be caused by our tendency to get comfortable on someone's lap and then start washing.

Humans are terribly coy about cleaning. They don't like others to watch them wash. I have known people close the bathroom door just to wash their hands, and then take quite a long time, with sounds of flushing and all. We cats are not at all self-conscious about our natural bodily functions.

When it is time for a bath, what we do is get up on a lap, claw and knead a little until things are smoothed just right, then settle in a carefully-balanced position. We may start by washing our faces (this, for some reason, brings about a response without fail – 'Oh look – he's washing his face!' Duh! Don't you?). After a while, we will delicately lift a leg and get to grips with any carelessness about our posteriors. As you can imagine, this sometimes takes quite a bit of effort, licking and cleaning, because we are very fussy about hygiene. It may be this that gives rise to those comments about our social manners. They judge us by their over-modest standards. I don't mind, really, because they will still love me.

The most important thing to a cat is to be loved, and it's not okay to be loved conditionally. We need to know that we are **loved unconditionally**, whatever we do. If you only love me when I am doing something cute like washing behind my ears, or keeping my bum out of sight, what kind of love is that?

Humans are really bothered about what is socially acceptable or unacceptable. They feel obliged to wear a mask of social respectability, as if their darlings would stop loving them if they revealed their real selves. They watch what they say, what they do and even how they walk and sit for fear of crossing some invisible, unwritten boundary that may well not even exist.

Silly people!

If someone really loves you, they accept your daily routine. They are only too glad that you are clean about your person even if you don't smell like some expensive perfume. Margaret sometimes buries her nose in my fur just for what she calls my 'cat smell'. Of course I smell like a cat – I **am** a cat! She loves me even when she's cross with me, like when I sit on her chest and she can't see the screen of her laptop, or when I draw blood with my claws. She loves me when I stick my backside in her face while I consider how I want to sit. She loves me because I am loveable. I am her cat!

I know this because she has told me, and I choose to believe her. There is absolutely no way that I would doubt her on such a fundamentally important matter. And if she loved me last year, she loves me now. Stands to reason, doesn't it?

I just wish I could share these thoughts with those poor, worried, tense, unbelieving humans who keep choosing to doubt perfectly truthful people's love. They get so worried about the possibility of losing their love that they can't risk what they believe might be socially unacceptable.

Weird.

CHAPTER 6

Cats care for their bodies

Now here's another thing. People have created a huge difference between their work and what they call 'time off'. This time out is a source of deep guilt and anxiety because of all the rules they like to attach to it; and these rules keep changing. I think someone makes a rule, everyone speaks about it and it becomes very fashionable to support it; but if it doesn't suit them, they quietly don't keep it. Then they will probably feel awfully guilty about it, as if they had broken a really important moral law.

Let me illustrate this.

One suggested rule is that people need to spend half an hour every day doing vigorous exercise so that their hearts keep fit. This leads to the use of a great amount of what I call the *obligation* words – 'should', 'must', 'ought' – that they use to beat themselves up with. Cats don't do that. If we want to run around, we do. If we want to sleep all day AND all night, we do. We just don't need to match each other, so we don't invent rules. If it's what my body wants now, I do it. If not, I don't do it.

Then there are those people who are always talking about it, as if all the talking could be the same as the actual deed! They keep fussing about "I should go and exercise!" or "I must join a gym" or whatever. And then they sit down and wait to forget the thought, while they have another cup of coffee and eat a bun. Then they say, "Oh my goodness, look at the time! It's far too late to exercise now!" And so their lives go by. Perhaps they don't want to go and exercise because they are tired from lack of sleep. They complain about being so tired, yet they don't do the obvious thing and just go and sleep.

Tommy in Study   MF

Do as we cats do. Nap. That's why we always have energy and never mind if you interrupt our snoozes. We know there's plenty more where that came from.

That's not how it is with humans. When they DO get to lie down and snooze, they are very sensitive about being woken up. Just look at what happens with humans if one comes to visit others soon after lunch on a Sunday while they are having a nap.

"I'm sorry – did I wake you?" Of course you did, silly person – what do you think Sunday afternoons are for?

"No, no, of course not!" No one believes that, looking at your crumpled face, but it would be SO embarrassing to admit that you were having a little lie-down.

Why 'little lie-down'? Why not big fat hibernate? Why embarrassing?

It's really quite simple. You do what your body wants. That way, your body knows that you and it are on the same side. I mean, no-one would be so stupid as to do something that was not good for them, surely? People have very advanced brains and can do maths and DIY and have deep conversations, so you would think they would be able to work this out for themselves.

But I often hear people saying, "I really shouldn't eat this!" and then they do. Or they have to reach for the white tablets they suck for acid in their tummies because they had too much to eat or drink. Overindulging is another mad thing they do.

If we cats have a moment around something too delicious to handle and find we have overindulged, we know what to do. We munch a bit of grass, bring up the excess and go to sleep. No problem.

Generally, however, we just take what we need and leave the rest.

But that's a side issue. I meant to talk about balance in life.

Personally, I like to get around 18 hours of sleep a day. You see, when I am awake, I don't mess around. I MOVE! I bounce, jump, stalk and pounce, run in

sudden bursts, climb up and down things in quick succession and get my heart rate right up. Then, of course, I need a rest again. Resting is not something to be ashamed of! It is just sensible.

The idea we have of life is principally that it should, as far as possible, be enjoyable. Humans are less fussy and vary their experiences. Sometimes they like to enjoy life, and sometimes they like to get upset and hate life.

Look at how they can work themselves into a fury about something someone else has done or said, and say, "I really don't need this in my life!" followed by time spent going over all the horrible aspects of whatever it is. What I don't understand is, if they really don't need it in their lives, why do they accept it?

We cats, if we don't like what someone is doing or saying to us, first just turn our backs, and if they don't stop, we up and walk away. If we don't need it in our lives, we don't have it. Simple as that.

And if we do need it, we get it.

Like these people and holidays. Everyone knows that humans are designed to run reasonably well for six days at around 16 hours a day, and then have to have a 24-hour break. Design specification. Without it, they get moody, bad-tempered, forgetful, inefficient and, often, sick.

They also need to have a change every now and then. Some to go away, some to stay at home and not have to go to work or school. I don't need holidays. In fact, I strongly dislike being anywhere except on my own territory. But people need to have these things.

Now you would think that, knowing all this (and they DO know it), they would have the brain power to take the time off, both each week and during the year. But do they? Many don't.

They blame their employers, the economy, their families, in fact anyone they can except themselves. Strangely, some of them are vain enough to think that if they go away or take the day off, the whole of society will collapse. Of course they would never admit to being conceited. They would have us believe that it's others that won't allow them to take time off, rather than their egos.

We know we are optional extras in urban society, we know that time off is essential to a cat's wellbeing, and we never confuse being needed with being loved. We just listen to our bodies, and when it's time to rest, we rest. When it's time to run and play, we do that.

If this is the only body I am going to have, I will look after it, and take that responsibility myself. That's where humans and cats differ.

CHAPTER 7

Cats are sensitive

it may sound to you as if I have been unnecessarily critical of people, and maybe you are thinking that I don't even like them.

You would be SO wrong. I love people. I care deeply about them. Even those who don't belong to me. You see, cats are very, very sensitive to people's emotions.

At the church, I regard it as my duty (and pleasure) to welcome people, make them feel at home, spend a bit of time with each and see how they are.

I walk around on Sunday mornings looking to see who is attending. There are some who come every single week and if they are not there I worry a little because there must be something wrong. Some come only from time to time, and I know who these are, so I don't mind when they are not there.

I check up on them all, spending a bit of time with each, and a little more with those who are emotionally 'open' – sometimes because they are sad or distressed, sometimes because they are lonely; sometimes just because they love cats. Of course, you always get the one who is not keen on cats. I make a special effort to spend extra time with them and keep on and on going back in spite of their insults because I believe that if they really got to know me, they would have to love me.

I don't confine my caring ministrations to Sunday services only. I also do funerals and weddings: sometimes I get invited to be in the wedding pictures, too. I like to attend everything that happens at the church all through the week. You would be surprised how many needy people come to the other programmes!

On Mondays, I pop in at the Yoga class to stretch a bit with them and give them some encouragement. I don't know what it is about Mondays, but this is the least cheerful class of the week. People seem to have so much more trouble stretching than cats do, and especially on Mondays!

Tuesday evenings I have the Prayer Meeting where they sing and pray very loudly indeed. Some of the members work in houses nearby and I visit them while they are cleaning, just now and then.

Wednesday evenings is Narcotics Anonymous and these meetings are always packed with great people, and very, very friendly. All ages, a mixture of every kind, but often distressed. I need to sit on laps a lot here, and sometimes I hardly have time to get round to all who need me.

Thursday mornings after yoga, is either Flower Club or University of the Third Age. Both involve a lot of elderly people and I have to watch out for walking sticks. At least the Flower Club has some young people, and both serve excellent teas.

In between are the various church meetings, some in the Rectory, and I like to be in on the Parish Council decisions, and check up from time to time on the Archdeaconry meetings. More good teas.

I understand that Amy used to do much the same before I came on the scene. . But then she is getting on in years, and there really is no need for her to do this now I have arrived. I made this very plain to her straight away, and just sent her packing. Now she also accepts that the church and the hall are entirely my territory and spends her time lying in the sun in the garden, or occupying Margaret's bed. Very restful.

I have heard some very cute little stories about Amy.   There is one story which I love hearing Margaret tell about the first time she experienced a funeral.

Amy had become very devout, so much so that she was affectionately known as an Anglicat.

This Thursday afternoon, the coffin was set up in front of the Sanctuary, a candle on either side, and a large, voluptuous arrangement of flowers somewhat precariously balanced on a wobbly palm stand to the right.

The mourners gathered and the church filled up. I started the service, the prayers were said and the eulogy delivered. After the reading I began the sermon, always slightly difficult when the late lamented has not been known to one.

Not far into the talk, Amy stalked down the centre aisle. I could see her inspecting each row of people, recognising this one and that, and wondering about the number of strangers suddenly in her church.

Gradually she worked her way down to the front. Suddenly she stopped. A silver stand with wheels? Something large and wooden on top? What on earth was this?

Delicately she applied her kitty nose and sniffed. First one corner and then another. A long, identifying sniff in the middle.

By now all eyes were on her. I am sure that if I had read the telephone directory aloud just then, no one would have noticed. Sniff, sniff round the lower edge of the coffin, lifting her front paws off the ground to get a better whiff of something new. My horror grew. I had no way of knowing what she might do next. I battled to keep the thread of the sermon.

Just as she rounded the second corner, she caught sight of the flower arrangement, with its lilies, chrysanthemums, carnations and ...gypsophylla! Now Amy has a passion for gypsophylla not unlike my feeling for chocolate.

This gypsophylla had been placed in a descending position, pouring out from the lower edges of the arrangement. She left the coffin, interesting as it was, and advanced on the flowers.

Carefully she stretched up, placed one little white paw high up against the leg of the stand and reached for the small flowers with the other. As she did so, the stand swayed slightly, the top wobbled and the arrangement teetered.

The congregation held its breath. I slowed down a bit. Amy tried again, her claws velveted within the immaculate white glove of her paw, gently reaching with cupped hand to catch the wonderful little flowers.

Again, the arrangement wobbled. I wondered whether to step sideways and pull a piece out for her and let her eat it quietly on the floor, or

whether to continue pretending nothing was amiss.
I hesitated, talking even more slowly. The
congregation watched, breathless. The moment
seemed frozen.

The paw still reached, the stand still
swayed, the top still wobbled and the arrangement
lurched. At the moment I decided the flowers HAD
to fall, Amy managed to snag a spray of
gypsophylla. Triumphant, she tugged it down on to
the floor and began to eat, pulling the small white
heads off the stalks.

All eyes slowly returned to me and together
we floundered on, looking for a decent way to end.
We had been through a deep emotional experience
together and we were united in our relief.

I said "Amen".

Amy licked her lips hugely, examined a paw
and began to clean her fur.

The congregation sang a hymn.

Order was restored and all was once again dignified and proper.

I wonder sometimes whether those who have gone before laugh at us as we solemnly follow our rituals, each time being careful to do all the things as they should be done, not to be seen to have shown less respect than anyone else. I wonder if they whisper into cat's ears and send them on their mission to enchant, to disrupt, and to entertain.

Now of course I would never have done anything so mindless.

However, I have been known to tear down the centre of the aisle, right up to the altar without stopping, only braking when I discover that it is solid wood and I cannot get to Margaret by going underneath the cloth. I find it quite amusing then to walk slowly sideways underneath the altar frontal with only my white paws and black tail tip showing until I get a whisker or two out at the side. Then I wait and sniff, to make sure that

everyone has quite caught up with me before I come out, nip round to behind the altar and do a quick jump up on to the reredos panelling behind.

There are six very tall candles there, and I like to do a slow slalom between them.

This tends to lift the mood of the service and to keep the children happy in particular. In fact, one family who divide their time between the Catholic and Anglican churches, began to prefer to come to my church just because of me.

I do get the feeling that some of the congregation are not paying full attention, while some are just SO serious and even a bit bound by tradition. They need me to get them focused again, and to remind them that worship is about joy and laughter in the presence of God.

After all, who was it that invented fun?

CHAPTER 8

Cats are charming

Margaret went away. For three months. And she left me with a man called David. She promised me that he would look after me and that all would be well.

But what she didn't tell me was that David DID NOT LIKE CATS.

In fact, he pushed me away quite hard when I came anywhere near him, and firmly closed the door to his room so that I couldn't keep him company and comfort him while he was living all alone in the rectory.

I hadn't met anyone who was quite so openly averse to us felines before and it was a challenge I could not resist.

But how to set about winning him over?

We cats are known to be bundles of charm, but if someone will not even allow you close enough to turn your great green eyes on him and gently purr, what do you do?

I kept up the charm offensive as much as I was able for several days, putting up with the closed doors and being shooed away with as much grace as I could muster. I wondered if Amy would be a better bet for softening the man's heart, but when I had observed David and Amy's interactions, I decided not.

Amy is, as I have told you, an old lady. She is not as bold as she used to be, and she prefers to be inside pretty well all the time now. This means that she has to have a litter tray inside. She eats the same food as I do, but something inside that aged interior transforms that food into a substance that smells so horrible that few living beings can be near it without being ill.

This, as you can imagine, just served to reinforce David's conviction that cats are not creatures one wants to spend time with.

Then there is the matter of Amy's feelings of insecurity which cause her to grip firmly with her claws, wherever she is. People don't like that, and the few times she tried to sit on David's lap, she got thrown across the room for her efforts.

Like many old ladies, she likes to have her own way, however, and it took a bit of time for David to convince her that he was never in this lifetime going to have her on his lap.

This was probably just as well, because if he had let her on for a while, he would have discovered her smelly breath too, and that would have set my programme back somewhat further.

As it was, I had quite a challenge on my hands.

What I did in the end was just talk soothingly to David whenever the opportunity arose. When it was time for food, for instance, I would murmur in a confidential, man-to-man sort of way, and he would oblige. A loud purr of appreciation was then needed, along with a glance from the big eyes. Gradually he began to talk back to me, and we set up quite an understanding.

Not that I could ever sit on him, of course. David is a very private man and does not like anyone in his personal space, so I learnt to respect that, though every now and again I tried to get close, just to check.

I think my gentle, patient approach worked well.

Humans, on the other hand, often seem to be in a rush to get things sorted out and defined. Some don't know what to do with a relationship once it has been defined, but they cannot sit still until that has been done. They seem to need verbal reassurance of permanent attachment. "Do you love me?" they ask. "Where is this leading?"

We cats like to reach the point of comfortable closeness then enjoy that. After all, when you think about it, life is made up of millions of moments in which one wishes to be happily comfortable, and if you have found someone who provides you with a sympathetic ear, a comfortable lap, some affectionate stroking and regular food, what more could you possibly want?

If it's not going to last forever, there is even more reason to make the most of it now and enjoy as much as you can get. And we make the most of what we have.

David wasn't very promising, but he was in the house, so I made do with him, and really got very fond of him.

I believe he got fond of me too – I know he spoke to me very lovingly by the time he had to leave.

CHAPTER 9

Catfights

Have you noticed that when cats fight, we never do so quietly?

Over the centuries, we cats developed a keen sense of community, and we tended to watch out for each other. That is, we watched out for the others in our own pack, pride or what you might call a clan.

Now that we tend to be so much more individual, attached to only one household at a time, we are much more vulnerable. We have no support other than our humans. And they sleep all night instead of keeping a watchful eye on our adventures. So when trouble strikes, we have to alert them to their duty of support.

I have mentioned Pepe before, and the way he likes to come onto my territory, spray all over and generally behave as if he owned the place. Well, from time to time we have it out, usually in the shrubbery just under Margaret's window – I would not be so foolish as to fight him at any distance from the Rectory – I know that she hates running barefoot in the street at night.

I must say, though, that she is immediate in her response. As soon as I begin the yowling, her light snaps on and she starts shouting. If that doesn't work, she is at the front door, unlocking all the security and in two ticks she has found us and is hissing and throwing things at him. He always gives up and runs away, and I have to stand and growl for a few minutes to make my point before retreating inside for a cuddle and some reassurance.

It is no fun to fight alone.

Humans, of course, are not always so clever, and many is the time they appear to go into battle unsupported. Certainly they can be very quiet about it – at least the ones at the church are. Sometimes you can sense that something is not right, but they say nothing. At least, they say nothing to the person concerned. They are not above relaying their version of the disagreement to others, though.

There are exceptions. We have a whole string of people who come to the door regularly for their food. They like to come one or two at  a time so as to make a long stream of doorbell rings. They wait until Margaret has settled down to do something and then the next one comes. I have seen them round the corner, comparing notes and food.

Unfortunately not all these people are sweet-tempered. When they get cross with each other - and believe me, they do! – they set about their fights just as we cats do. They have obviously learnt from us that the more attention you attract, the more support you are likely to get.

So they make a huge noise. They can outscream any cat any night of the week using most unusual words to express themselves probably on the basis that one should use fighting language when attacking and defending. They also often push each other, punch each other, and fall over a lot.

Margaret's response is just as quick as when I fight, with the light going on and her shouting through the window. Mind you, she only comes outside for me. **They** have to sort themselves out. Once or twice she has asked the police to give them a hand, and the police are always very happy to oblige.

What I have noticed is that these people are good friends again soon afterwards. Those who grit their teeth and keep quiet about their upsets tend to avoid each other for much longer - sometimes months or even years. It's probably a good idea to bring things into the light and have a good fight from time to time, just to remind everyone about who's who, and how far one's territory extends.

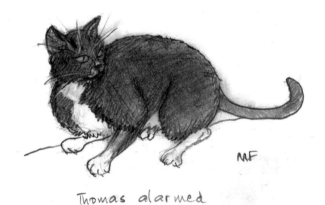

Thomas alarmed

CHAPTER 10

Cats are survivors

They say cats have nine lives. Why only nine? I think we may have as many lives as we want.

We are seriously not afraid to die, and when life gets too difficult or too painful, it's generally a good idea to leave it and go on to the next life, so we find a hospitable bush, lie down under it and quietly expire. Until then we might as well get down to some serious enjoyment. And when you making the most of every moment, you are inclined to hold on to this life at all costs.

To enable you to hold on to and enjoy your life, here are four Cat Principles:

Firstly, BE RELAXED. There is absolutely nothing to be gained by tensing up. Imagine you have made a mistake in choosing the branch you are on high up a tree. As it breaks and you realise that you are on your way down, making your body tense is hardly going to stop your fall, is it? It's not going to soften anything on the way, or prepare your body for impact either.

On the other hand, if you let all your muscles go soft and think to yourself, "Whee! I am  flying!" then you achieve two things. First, you really enjoy the moment so that if something dreadful happens, at least you die happy; second, your muscles are so soft that they are like cushions for your bones, and they are less likely to break. I have known cats who fell from several storeys up and still walked away relatively comfortably – bruised but not broken.

Now this is good advice, both in the literal and the figurative sense. When you find that your support or your security is collapsing, don't get tense – it only takes the blood supply away from your brain into your tense muscles and then not only do you make poor decisions, you probably also get muscle spasms and a sore neck.

Relax. Grab whatever you can in the moment. You may never have another like it! And if you have to make a big decision, get excited – it's not every day you have the opportunity to choose a major direction. Crises are so liberating and full of amazing possibilities. Don't waste any one of them.

Secondly, TAKE TIME TO RECOVER. When something unusual, hurtful or damaging happens to you, immediately opt out for a while and allow your system to settle around the new situation. I like to find a patch of sunshine, or in winter a place next to the fire, to curl up and snooze for a day or two. It allows my brain to operate without having to manage the body at the same time.

Now there are people who seem to go into overdrive when something bad happens. The first thing they like to do is tell everyone that they're okay. The worse the disaster, the more they discount it. Then they go to great lengths to carry on as usual, or, if they can, even better.

I haven't yet found out why this is. I would think they would want sympathy and gentling, but they only consent to that if problem is something really small. Like if something spills on a new piece of clothing, then they behave as if it is a disaster. Or if one of them has a cold, they want friends to rally round, maybe with chicken soup as if they were gravely ill. But just watch them when they have had a hip replacement – they will be cycling within the week if they have a bicycle. All to prove how stoic and strong they are.

Wouldn't it be better if they did what the doctor said, and took proper time to recover? If they were laid off for a week, to take a week off and vegetate until the body has regrouped and is ready to go on.

Thirdly, as I've said before, EAT WHAT YOU NEED. You don't need to put anything into your body that you don't require for good health. If you don't have a home to support you and you need to grab whatever you can, please set about getting one. And once you have a good home, train the food supplier to get it right. Sniff, taste, consider, try it for a day and see what happens. If the food is not right, your body will tell you. Then, for goodness sake, *don't eat it*! There are so many different kinds of food that there is absolutely no need whatever to waste your time and effort with the wrong stuff. If necessary, rather eat nothing than the wrong food.

Now people really don't get this, and they put themselves at awful risk. Sometimes they even tempt us to join in, offering us chocolate, biscuits, even ice cream! Now give me a good, balanced pellet - nourishment, tooth cleaning and a good crunch all in one - and I am totally happy.

Lastly, let me repeat this: NEVER CROSS YOUR BRIDGES BEFORE YOU GET TO THEM. People like to imagine what disaster could possibly happen, then they live through this over and over in their imaginations until all their joy has gone. If it does happen, they have to live through it again in reality. If it doesn't, they have suffered countless times for nothing.

A cat would never do that.

For me, if everything is cool today, my life is completely satisfactory. I don't have to worry about tomorrow's possible disasters - which may or may not happen. All I have to deal with is what is now, in front of my wet nose. Of course, I do take sensible precautions to make sure that I will have the strength and health to meet tomorrow, but I don't ever dwell on the negative possibilities of life.

Some people are so busy worrying about imagined threats that they have no emotional energy left to handle the actual demands of real life. I find that difficult to understand.

It's all in the Bible anyway. Sometimes I think that perhaps God is also a cat. I mean, wasn't it God who said, "Take no thought for tomorrow"? And doesn't God keep trying to teach people to relax and rest and be present in their bodies? If they were to learn from us cats, they might begin to become the way are they are meant to be – just like God.

See, I do listen in church!

CHAPTER 11

Cats play

I've put this chapter near the end because this is possibly the key to our nature. You may have noticed that **every** cat plays whenever the opportunity arises. Well, until the cat reaches an age when everything except sleeping and eating has lost its attraction, that is.

Poor old Amy. She does a very chilly ignore when Margaret tries to tempt her to chase a piece of string. She looks at her accusingly as if to say, "Don't insult me. I'm now officially a Geriatricat, having passed 14 years of age **many** years ago." She requires respect from everyone now, even from me! (You probably know that cats are 100 in human terms soon after 14.)

Something I have noticed about some people is that they treat their children far worse than they treat their kittens. Put a kitten in their household and immediately everyone dances to its tune. It gets its food on time, and should it utter the tiniest "Miaow", everyone there jumps to see to it. And they spend hours playing with it. They ignore their own children a great deal, however, requiring them to fit in with the grown-up schedule and getting irritated when the children play happily and noisily.

You see, playing is essential to growth and development. Even when we are adult, we cats play a lot, because it hones our skills and keeps us fit and fast. Show me anything that moves and I will try to catch it. I even jump for birds, though I know there is very little chance of catching them on the wing!

I wish human parents would sit down and play with their little ones while they are tiny, and then encourage them to play a lot when they are bigger. So what if they make a noise? At least they are doing what young animals are supposed to do. Their parents should be glad and happy to join in. Instead of that, I've heard them say, "Oh grow up", or, "I can't wait for you to be old enough to …"

If children were encouraged to play more, perhaps they would achieve more. I hear parents pushing children to "do their best", "concentrate", "work harder" instead of letting them play their way to success.

Am I glad I am a cat! Imagine cat mothers getting together and saying, "My kitten can walk on his back paws already!", or "My kitten can recognise catfood commercials on TV!"

So my wish for human children is that they be allowed to be children for as long a time as possible, and that they be encouraged to play, often, just like cats.

Finally

As you can see, I've given all this a lot of thought. Don't for a moment think that cats' minds are blank when we lie in the sun or curl up in front of a fire. We are, with some notable exceptions, very deep.

The conclusion I have reached is this: Cats know that we are not on this earth for all that long, so we make the most of every moment. We minimise thoughts and activities that consume our emotional energy with no positive results, and maximise those that bring enjoyment and satisfaction - and if not to ourselves, then to someone we love. People could also do this, and they could live in the moment and treasure each second as we do, if they really wanted to. They could make a study of cats and do their best to emulate us. Just imagine what the world would be like if they did!

Good luck, reader: I hope you have a lovely cat to guide you.